Claims for In

A Practitioner's Guide

Industrial Diseases Series

Claims for Industrial Deafness

A Practitioner's Guide

His Honour Judge
Alistair MacDuff QC

CLT Professional Publishing
A Division of Central Law Training Ltd

© Alistair MacDuff 1997

Published by
CLT Professional Publishing
A division of Central Law Training Ltd
Wrens Court
52/54 Victoria Road
Sutton Coldfield
Birmingham B72 1SX

ISBN 1 85811 123 4

Produced by Palladian, PO Box 15, Bembridge

Typeset by Adrian McLaughlin
Printed in Great Britain by The Looseleaf Company

Contents

Introduction

Claims for damages in respect of noise-induced deafness, arising out of a plaintiff's employment, are no different from other claims for personal injury. The intended plaintiff must, as in all cases, establish, on the balance of probabilities, the essential ingredients of his claim; (i) that the defendants exposed him to noise; (ii) that the defendants were negligent, alternatively that there was some breach of statutory duty; and (iii) that he has suffered a hearing loss as a result of that exposure to noise. Negligence must be established in the normal way; the defendants should reasonably have foreseen that the exposure to noise was so great (duration of time and noise intensity) as to be liable to cause injury, and they were in breach of their duty of care. Nevertheless, the inexperienced practitioner, instructed to handle a deafness case for the first time, requires a helping hand. The terminology needs to be understood. The practitioner will need to know how to assess the medical evidence, how to calculate noise levels, and how to assess the evidence generally.

This Guide is intended to provide assistance for the first time or inexperienced practitioner in handling a deafness claim, whether on behalf of the plaintiff or the defendants; it aims to provide, in digestible nutshell form, the basic information which the practitioner will need. He will, of course, need to build upon this; but it is hoped and intended that this Guide will provide the material to enable him to take the first (and most difficult) step towards becoming a specialist in this field.

It is intended that this should be the book which I would have liked to have been available all those years ago when I made my own first tentative steps as a PI practitioner and drafted my first deafness Particulars of Claim. A draft Particulars of Claim has been provided as an Appendix. It may be adapted, as appropriate.

Alistair MacDuff
March 1997

Chapter 1

Foreseeability

It has been known for many years, going back into the last century, that heavy industrial noise would cause deafness. Those working in ship-building and ship-repairing, drop forging, stamping and other heavy manufacturing industries would, almost inevitably, become significantly deaf in middle age. There is much documentation to establish that both employers and workmen, in these heavy industries, were aware, as a matter of common sense, that excessive noise and deafness were linked. But this risk was accepted by employers and workmen alike, and nothing was done about it. Not until the 1970s did the Factory Inspectorate (Health and Safety Executive) take any interest. Deafness only became a prescribed disease as recently as 1975. Almost without exception, employers, even in the heaviest and noisiest industries, did not begin to provide ear protection until after 1970.

When industrial deafness cases first came before the courts, there was plenty of available evidence to show that the reasonable employer (at least in the heaviest and noisiest industries) should have foreseen the risk of injury many years ago. However, in the leading reported case of *Thompson* v *Smiths Ship Repairers Limited* [1984] 1 All ER 881, Mustill J determined the date of foreseeability as 1963. This coincided with the publication of the Safety Health & Welfare Booklet "Noise and the Worker". Before 1963, an employer would not be negligent in failing to provide hearing protection for his workforce; after 1963, the employer had a positive duty to do so.

In fact, Mustill J did not hold that the danger was not foreseeable prior to 1963. Rather he held that the reasonable employer was not under any duty to provide protection until after that date. It is not necessary, in this book, to explore the rationale of the decision. It is sufficient to note that, for all practical purposes, an employer who exposed his workforce to excessive noise prior to 1963 was not negligent; an employee who was exposed to excessive noise after 1963 will have a valid claim.

The case of *Thompson* was decided upon the basis of what the reasonable employer knew or should have known in the light of published material. If a plaintiff can establish that his own employer *in fact* had special knowledge prior to 1963, it may be possible to establish liability from an earlier date. Such a case was *Kellett v. British Rail Engineering Limited* (1984) a decision of Popplewell J, which is unreported. In that case, the defendants disclosed documents upon discovery which showed that they had been actively considering the problem of noise-induced deafness from the early 1950s. They had special additional knowledge, and their Chief Medical Officer had been urging the purchase of ear protectors. The learned judge said,

> "If the plaintiff's case depended solely on the published literature produced I would have been inclined to adopt the same view as Mr Justice Mustill (in *Thompson*) ... that 1963 was about the date when the defendants should be found liable, and for the same reasons. In the instant case, however, the documents disclosed by the defendants show not merely that the defendants from about 1951 had the means of knowledge, but that they actually knew of the risk involved. They knew what precautions should be taken and what protection was available, yet so far as this plaintiff was concerned they took no steps at all ...".

He then went on to hold that the defendants should have provided protection for the plaintiff by 1955, at the latest.

In summary, in the vast majority of deafness cases, 1963 will be taken as the date of knowledge. In a small number of cases, if it can be shown that the defendants had additional *actual* knowledge, it may be possible to establish an earlier date of foreseeability.

Chapter 2

Understanding the terminology

Perhaps the biggest difficulty for a busy practitioner, instructed in an industrial deafness case for the first time, is to understand the documents. Noise intensity is measured in decibels. Noise is conducted through the air in wave-like agitations of different frequencies (or different wavelengths) which are measured in hertz. The practitioner will need to understand the concept of the "A-weighted" decibel and he will also need to understand how a "noise dose" may be calculated by use of the symbol Leq.

Decibel (db or dB)

This is a measurement of noise pressure level. For practical purposes it may be considered as a measure of "loudness". The higher the db reading, the louder the noise. Obviously, as noise passes through the air it becomes progressively softer. The closer the ear to the source of noise, the louder it will be. Thus where noise is measured (in decibels) by use of a noise meter, it is important to ensure that the instrument is accurately positioned.

Hertz (hz) and kilohertz (khz)

As has already been stated, noise is conducted through the air in waves of differing lengths. These waves may be measured either in length or frequency. Long wavelengths will have low frequency; short wavelengths have higher frequencies. The basic unit of frequency is one cycle per second, or one hertz. 1000 hz equals 1 khz. High pitched noise (for example the top end of a piano) is relatively high frequency noise. Low pitched noise (the bass notes on a piano) are of low frequency. Human speech is conveyed within the range of frequencies between 0.25 khz and 4 khz.

Thus, it is important to understand that the human ear receives sounds across a wide range of frequencies from the very low frequency (the bass notes in a piece of music) to the very high (for example birdsong). At any given moment, it is likely that the human ear will be receiving a mixture of sounds across a broad range of frequencies. This is true in the factory environment. The human ear is being assailed by a "package" of sound in numerous frequencies, measured in hertz or kilohertz. Indeed, very few sounds experienced in everyday life consist of a single pure tone. Almost always sounds are composed of a mixture of frequencies across a wide range.

A-weighted decibels (dbA or dBA)

It is known that the human ear is more vulnerable to injury from noise which it receives within the range 1 kz to 4 kz. It is also known that prolonged exposure to noise (within that range of frequencies) in excess of 90 db is liable to result in hearing loss to the average person. That is to say, if the human ear is constantly bombarded with noise in excess of 90 decibels and within the frequencies 1–4 khz, it is probable that deafness will result. However, at lower frequencies (say 0.5 khz) and at higher frequencies (say 6 khz) the human ear is not so vulnerable. Noise in these low and high frequencies is subjectively less "loud", even though the noise pressure levels may considerably exceed 90 db. At these low and high frequencies, noise levels of, say, 96 decibels might be necessary before the human ear is exposed to risk of injury. Accordingly, noise meters are manufactured which give differential weight to the measured sound levels, so as to give a figure reflecting a notional response of a human ear. The noise meter receives all sounds over all frequencies, measures their intensity in decibels, giving more significance to sound within the middle (more harmful) frequencies, so as to produce an overall measurement described as "A-weighted decibels" or dBA, thus making an allowance for the fact that sounds in the lower and higher frequencies are less harmful to the ear.

LEQ

At this stage, it becomes necessary to calculate what may be termed the "noise dose". Thus far, we have considered noise "loudness" (decibels) and wavelengths/frequencies (kilohertz). When one calculates whether a particular worker is at risk, the *duration of exposure* is also important. Obviously, a person who is exposed to noise levels of 90 dBA continuously for eight hours per day and five days per week is more likely to be at risk than some other worker who is exposed to the same noise levels for a shorter period (either because the noise is only intermittent, or because he/she only works part-time). Accordingly, means have been developed of arriving at an equivalent continuous sound level, denoted by the symbol Leq. This is the notional sound level which, in the course of an eight-hour period, would cause the same A-weighted sound energy to be recorded as that due to the actual sound over the actual working day.

Thus, Leq takes account of the duration of noise exposure. Worker A works for eight hours per day, five days per week, in a noise environment measured at 90 dBA. His Leq is necessarily 90 dBA. This is because he actually works a 40-hour week in a constant noise environment measured at 90 dBA.

Worker B, on the other hand, is exposed to noise only intermittently. He also works eight hours per day and five days per week. But noise levels, in his case, are measured at 93 dBA (for example) for 50% of his time at work. For the remaining half of his time, noise levels are, say, only 87 dBA. The modern noise meter will be able to translate all that information to produce a "noise dose" which might also measure 90 dBA Leq.

Thus, it will be appreciated that worker B has suffered exactly the same "noise dose" as worker A, though he has received it in a different way.

Worker C, on the other hand, might be exposed to even higher levels of noise but for shorter periods of time. Let us assume levels of noise intensity measuring as much as 95 dBA but only on rare occasions during the working day. During the majority of the working day, however, noise levels are relatively low, let us assume 75 dBA or 80 dBA. Worker C's "noise dose" would be considerably lower than that of worker A or worker B, even though, on occasions, he has been exposed to the loudest noise.

Chapter 3

Breach of the Duty of Care

It is now well established that the "watershed" between risk and safety is defined at 90 dBA Leq. As we have seen above, it is known that prolonged exposure to noise in excess of 90 dB is liable to result in hearing loss to the average person. In fact, some people are more vulnerable to noise than others. All human ears are not identical. A relatively small number of people may suffer injury from a noise dose of less than 90 dBA Leq. Others may have extra resilience; they may be able to cope with regular noise in excess of 90 dBA. However, the courts have held that 90 dBA Leq is the dividing line between risk and safety. If the worker (plaintiff) proves that the employer (defendant) exposed him to a "noise dose" of 90 dBA Leq or higher, his claim will succeed. That is to say, the plaintiff must prove that he was exposed to the equivalent of noise in excess of 90 A-weighted decibels for 40 hours per week.

Clearly, the burden of proof is upon the plaintiff. He must prove that he was exposed to excessive levels of noise, that is to say that his "noise dose", calculated as above, exceeded 90 dBA Leq. If the factory is still in production an acoustics expert engineer may be instructed to take noise meter readings and to make the necessary calculations. Of course, allowance will be made for any changes which have occurred during the relevant period of employment. Production processes may have changed. Old machines may have been replaced by new machines. The expert may need to make adjustments to the figures to take account of these changes. The plaintiff and fellow employees may give evidence as to the effects of change describing how the factory was busier, noisier, etc in early years. The expert will make allowance for these changes, and (where, for example, old noisy machinery has been made redundant) he may have taken noise measurements of similar machinery in the past when making an inspection at other factory premises. In such cases, where adjustments have to be made, it may become a matter of evidence as to whether, on the balance of probabilities, the "watershed" of 90 dBA Leq has been crossed.

Discovery also assumes great importance. As has been stated earlier, industrial noise became an issue in the early 1970s. At that time, the HSE issued a code of practice (1972). Much publicity was given to the need to protect factory workers from excessive noise. Many engineering and other employers commissioned their own noise surveys (often at the behest of the HSE) to determine whether there was a noise problem. If so, the results of those surveys would be discloseable upon discovery. Such surveys could be interpreted by an acoustics expert with the help of the plaintiff's own evidence. Many of the surveys will have been undertaken using older and less sophisticated equipment, which will not translate (for example) noise level measurements from dB into dBA. Using the plaintiff's own evidence (where he used to work within the factory; how far distant from machines A and B; for how many hours per day; and how often were the machines operating etc) the acoustics expert will be able to use the old noise survey to make a reasonably accurate assessment of the plaintiff's "noise dose", measured in dBA Leq.

In order to discharge his duty of care, the employer is under an obligation to provide ear protection. In some cases, adjustments to machinery, or the introduction of baffles or other noise suppressing equipment can result in a substantial reduction in noise levels. In the vast majority of cases, the employer will provide ear defenders and will enforce their use in those areas of the factory where noise exceeds 90 dBA. In practice, industry in general did not take these steps until the early to mid 1970s. It is for the plaintiff to prove, by factual and expert evidence, that he was receiving a "noise dose" in excess of 90 dBA Leq during the period after 1963 and the time when ear protection was provided.

Chapter 4

Understanding the Audiogram

A typical audiogram is reproduced at Figure 1. The same information is set out in tabular form in Figure 2.

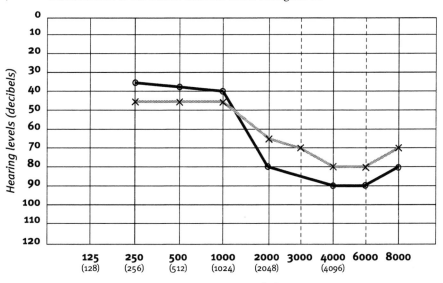

Key: ━━━ R   ∙∙∙∙∙∙∙∙ L

Figure 1

Frequency (hz)	R	L
250	35	45
1000	40	45
2000	80	65
3000	85	70
4000	90	80
6000	90	80
8000	80	70

Figure 2

The audiogram is used as a map of the threshold between hearing and deafness. As can be seen, frequencies are represented along the horizontal; and hearing level in the vertical. The subject (let us call him "the patient") is provided with earphones. A tone is played, and the patient is asked to say when he can discern the tone. Tones are played at different frequencies and at different noise intensity levels.

Let us examine the particular patient in Figure 1.

A tone would be played into the right ear at 250 hertz. The patient was unable to hear a tone played at 20 decibels or 30 decibels, but was able to discern the tone at 35 decibels and louder. The results in the right ear are mapped by the letter "O" and the results in the left ear by the letter "X". At 250 hertz, the left ear was unable to discern the tone played at less than 45 decibels. The right ear could begin to hear sound of 1 kilohertz frequency (1,000 hertz) when it reached 40 decibels. At 2,000 hertz, the right ear could only hear sounds of 80 or more decibels. And so on.

It will be appreciated that a person with absolutely perfect hearing would have a graph which ran horizontally along the top line, showing a nil decibel loss. It will also be appreciated that this particular patient has reasonably good hearing for sounds in the lower frequencies (250 hertz and 1,000 hertz) but has a substantial hearing loss for sounds at frequencies of 4 kilohertz and 6 kilohertz. Thus, the deafness is not uniform. This might be illustrated if one imagines this patient's listening to a piece of orchestral music. He would be able to hear the low notes and the bass section of the orchestra with ease, but would lose many of the higher notes of the flute and piano, particularly if those notes were played softly. Similarly, speech would be distorted. Deep vowel sounds would be heard relatively easily, whereas sibilant consonant sounds such as "s" and "t" would be missed. For example, the word "systems" if spoken softly or from some distance away could possibly sound like "iddem". This lack of uniformity in deafness is significant, because it cannot be cured by merely turning up the volume. Sophisticated hearing aids are now available which amplify certain frequencies more than others. But, without a hearing aid, a patient has to suffer a disabling distortion of speech and other sounds.

How accurate is the audiogram? After all, it relies upon the patient's own responses to whether or not he can hear a particular sound. A skilled otologist will be able to tell whether the patient is attempting to mislead. An audiogram is not taken merely by using one frequency and increasing the volume until the patient says he can hear. Frequencies and levels of intensity can be mixed and intermingled to detect the malingerer. Thus the malingerer may be induced into inconsistencies of response. Also, he can be tested at the same intensity and same frequency more than once.

Audiograms are normally undertaken by way of air conduction. That is to say, the tone is played directly into the ear and is conveyed to the ear drum (where it is subjectively heard) along the outer ear and ear canal. Audiograms may also be done by way of bone conduction. Here the sound is conveyed to the ear drum along the bony structures in the skull. In the normal case, the results will be similar, whether ear conduction or bone conduction is used. However, if the outer ear, including the ear canal is damaged, the patient may record better results on bone conduction. In such a case, the deafness is not caused by noise. Noise only attacks the hearing mechanisms of the ear drum itself causing damage which is said to be "sensori-neural". If there is conductive deafness (caused by damage to the conducting parts of the ear) as opposed to sensori-neural deafness, excessive noise cannot be the culprit. Damage to the conducting part of the ear may be caused by other injury or disease/infection of one sort or another.

Sometimes, inconsistencies in the audiogram (perhaps between air conduction and bone conduction) may cause the otologist to query whether the patient is genuine or may be exaggerating his disability. In such a case "invoked response audiometry" can be used as a diagnostic aid.

In summary, in all cases an expert otologist will be asked to examine the claimant and produce a report. An experienced otologist will be able to produce an audiogram, to confirm whether or not the audiogram is typical of noise-induced deafness, to confirm that the deafness is sensori-neural (and therefore likely to be noise-induced) and (if necessary) to say whether or not the claimant gave consistent and genuine responses so as to produce a reliable audiogram.

In fact, Figures 1 and 2 are typical of a case of noise-induced hearing loss. Typically, the greatest deafness is at frequencies between 4 and 6 kilohertz.

One further piece of information; whereas (as stated earlier) a person with absolutely perfect hearing would have a graph which ran horizontally along the top line of the audiogram, showing a nil decibel loss, it is generally accepted that, in the average person, there is no subjective deafness until the 20 decibel line has been reached. That is to say, there is a "reservoir" of hearing which may be tapped before a person can appreciate subjectively that his/her hearing is impaired. Subjectively, a person with a nil decibel loss and a person with, say, a 15/20 decibel loss have equally acute hearing. But the latter has lost his/her "reservoir" and will begin to become hard of hearing if there is any further damage. Again, we are discussing the average. Some will have a larger reservoir; others will experience subjective deafness with only, say, a 10 decibel loss.

Chapter 5

Calculating the Hearing Loss

A method has been developed for producing a shorthand statement of a patient's hearing loss. It enables a comparison to be made between different patients (and plaintiffs) and is therefore an aid when assessing the quantum of damages. The method of calculation is arbitrary and unsophisticated, but it does enable an assessment to be made of any individual patient's binaural (both ears) hearing loss. An average loss of hearing is calculated for each ear. That average loss is calculated by taking the decibel loss for each ear at three separate frequencies, and producing the average of those three figures. Traditionally, the three selected frequencies are 1 khz, 2 khz, and 3 khz. Many otologists believe, however, that a truer picture is obtained by averaging the losses at 1 khz, 2 khz and 4 khz. (For the purpose of industrial disablement benefit the former method of calculation is used.) In Figure 3, below, we can calculate the average loss for the patient whose audiogram is contained at Figures 1 and 2, above. As can be seen (using the first method of calculation 1 khz, 2 khz and 3 khz) the average loss in the right ear is 68.3 decibels; in the left ear it is 60 decibels. Using the second method (1 khz, 2 khz and 4 khz) the average loss in the right ear is 70 decibels and, in the left ear, is 63.3 decibels.

First Method		R	L		*Second Method*		R	L
Loss at	1 khz	40	45		Loss at	1 khz	40	45
	2 khz	80	65			2 khz	80	65
	3 khz	85	70			4 khz	90	80
		205	180				210	190

First method	average right ear:	205 ÷ 3	= 68.3 db
First method	average left ear:	180 ÷ 3	= 60 db
Second method	average right ear:	210 ÷ 3	= 70 db
Second method	average left ear:	190 ÷ 3	= 63.3 db

Figure 3

Next, it becomes necessary to calculate the binaural (both ears) average loss. Figure 4 shows how this is done. As can be seen, the calculation is weighted in that the better ear is taken four times, and is given more significance than the worse ear. This is because the better ear compensates substantially for the worse ear. For example, patient X may have excellent hearing in one ear, but be stone deaf in the other ear. Nevertheless, he can hear perfectly well with the good ear. He is much less disabled than patient Y who has a 50 per cent (for want of a better description) hearing loss in both ears. Because the better ear compensates the patient in this way, it is given more weight in the calculation. Figure 4 (using the same patient as Figure 3) shows how the binaural calculation is made.

Average binaural loss at 1, 2 and 3 khz
Right (worse) ear: 68.3 db.
Left (better) ear: 60 db x 4 = 240
(68.3 + 240) ÷ 5 =   61.6 db
                           Average binaural loss = 61.6 db

Average binaural loss at 1, 2 and 4 khz
Right (worse) ear: 70 db
Left (better) ear: 63.3 db x 4 = 253.2
(70 + 253.2) ÷ 5 =   64.6 db
                           Average binaural loss = 64.6 db

Figure 4

Chapter 6

Quantum

Apportionment

In *Thompson* v *Smiths Ship Repairers Limited* [1984] 1 All ER 881, the plaintiffs argued that they were suffering from an injury which was one and indivisible, and that the negligent defendants should be required to compensate the plaintiffs *in full* for the deafness which they had suffered. In that case, all the plaintiffs had been working in conditions of excessive noise for many years prior to 1963. As we have seen above, it was held that the defendants were only negligent from 1963 onwards. Nevertheless (it was argued on behalf of the plaintiffs) the defendants had made a material contribution to the plaintiffs' injuries, and should be held liable in damages for the whole of the plaintiffs' disabilities.

This submission followed the line of cases which includes *Bonnington Castings Ltd* v *Wardlaw* (1956) 1 All ER 615, *Nicholson* v. *Atlas Steel etc Ltd* [1957] 1 All ER 776 and *McGhee* v. *NCB* [1972] 3 All ER 1008. This submission was rejected by Mustill J.

> "I cannot think it legitimate for a plaintiff ... to recover in full for a loss, part of which is known to have occurred before the wrongful conduct began."

The court will apportion. Each individual defendant is only liable for that part of the injury which that defendant has caused. Thus, in *Thompson* the judge initially made a valuation of the individual cases as though *all* the damage had been caused negligently; he then discounted to reflect the fact that a proportion of the damage had been caused without negligence prior to 1963, when the defendants first became liable. This approach was followed by Popplewell J in the case of *Kellett* v *British Rail Engineering Ltd* (1984 unreported) to which we have already referred.

The same approach will be applied, of course, where there is more than one defendant. Where, for example, a plaintiff has been exposed to excessive noise by (say) three separate negligent employers, each employer will only be liable for the proportion of deafness caused by his relevant employment. The three employers would not be both jointly and severally liable for the full loss, with apportionment between them. The plaintiff must sue all three employers and (subject to proof of negligence) will receive the appropriate proportion of his total damages from each of those three.

The court will frequently be faced with the problem of how to discount for a pre-existing noise-induced deafness which the plaintiff had already suffered, either as the result of an earlier employment or before the date of foreseeability. In such cases, it is important to receive evidence from both the medical expert and the engineering expert as to the likely extent of the plaintiff's disability, if his hearing had been tested at the beginning of the relevant period of employment. The experts are able to make this assessment, albeit in approximate terms, from the evidence about noise levels, the durations of exposure, and statistics which would show how the average human ear would be likely to respond to those levels and durations of noise exposure.

It must also be borne in mind that the apportionment should not be undertaken on a straight pro rata basis. Let us take an example. Let us imagine a plaintiff with a binaural hearing loss of, say, 60 decibels. Let us assume that he has worked for the defendants, in excessive noise, for 15 years. Let us assume that the defendants are negligently responsible only for the most recent 10 years, and not for the first five years. Let us further assume that his presumed hearing loss 10 years ago, when the negligent employment began, is assessed at 20 decibels (average binaural loss) so that the defendants would be responsible for the deterioration (from 20 to 60 decibels) in an already disabled plaintiff. At first glance, it might seem appropriate to assess damages for the full 60 decibel loss and then discount by one-third. That would not be correct. Such a course would not give sufficient weight to the fact that to make a man already deaf still deafer is to increase his handicap very considerably, particularly as he has fewer decibels to spare. In a sense, the later decibels are more precious to the plaintiff.

There can be no precise approach to this question of apportionment. It is very much a matter of "feel" but assistance can be obtained from the judgments in the cases already mentioned (both *Thompson* and *Kellett*) and other decided cases.

Tinnitus

Many plaintiffs will experience tinnitus in addition to their deafness. This is a persistent, continuous or intermittent ringing/high pitched buzzing in the ear. Where it is continuous, it can be extremely distressing. Devices are now available which can, to some extent, mask the tinnitus, although these are of moderate value. Clearly, the extent and nature of the tinnitus must be considered when placing a valuation upon any given claim.

Assistance with quantification

At the present time (1997) a claim in respect of total deafness would be valued within the range £35,000 to £40,000. In the case of a young plaintiff with troublesome tinnitus, the award could be higher. That figure really sets the bench mark. It is possible to place any individual case within the appropriate tariff by calculating (if the medical expert has not already done this calculation) the binaural average loss of the particular plaintiff. Comparisons may then be made with other decided cases, and the relevant section in Kemp The *Quantum of Damages,* volume 2, contains details of many awards, with which comparisons may be made. An appropriate allowance must be made, one way or the other, to take account of any tinnitus, and whether such tinnitus is troublesome or mild, whether it is constant or intermittent. Of course, allowance must also be made for the passage of time and the fall in the value of money.

Chapter 7

Breach of Statutory Duty

In *Thompson* v *Smith's Ship Repairs Limited* [1984] 1 All ER 881 Mustill J decided that the defendants were not in breach of section 29(1) of the Factories Act 1961. This section imposes a duty upon the factory occupier to make and keep safe every place at which any person has at any time to work. It had been argued that the plaintiffs' places of work had not been made and kept safe in that noise levels gave rise to risk of injury. Whether or not there had been a breach of section 29(1) was of academic interest only; the judge held that negligence had been established. It was, perhaps, surprising that there had been no breach of statutory duty. If, as the Judge held, the plaintiffs had been exposed to foreseeable risk of injury, why were their places of work not unsafe?

In the unreported case of *Kellett* v *British Rail Engineering Limited* (1984) Popplewell J took a different view. He held that the employers were in breach of section 29(1).

It is not a matter of any great concern; this section of the Factories Act cannot add to the common law duty. It may be pleaded as a make-weight, but it cannot assist the plaintiff who is unable to establish negligence.

By regulation 44 of the Woodworking Machines Regulations 1974,

"Where any factory or any part thereof is mainly used for work carried out on woodworking machines, the following provisions shall apply to that factory or part as the case may be:
(a) where on any day any person employed is likely to be exposed continuously for 8 hours to a sound level of 90 dB(A) or is likely to be subject to an equivalent or greater exposure to sound (i) such measures as are reasonably practicable shall be taken to reduce noise to the greatest extent which is reasonably practicable and (ii) suitable ear protectors shall be provided and made readily available for the use of every such person.
(b) All ear protectors provided in pursuance of the foregoing paragraph shall be maintained and shall be used by the person for whom they are provided in any of the circumstances specified in

paragraph (a) of this Regulation.

(c)   For the purpose of paragraph (a) of these Regulations the level of exposure which is equivalent to or greater than continuous exposure for 8 hours to a sound level of 90 dB(A) shall be determined by an approved method."

The above Regulation, it is submitted, is, in effect, an accurate statement of the common law duty, established by such cases as *Thompson* and *Kellett*. It has limited application in that it only applied to factories where woodworking machines were being operated. It was in force from 1974 to 1989, when it was revoked by the Noise at Work Regulations 1989.

These 1989 Regulations came into force on 1 January 1990. Thus, they assist the practitioner only in those cases where there has been exposure to noise after that date. Once again, the "watershed" is set at 90 dB(A). A daily exposure level in excess of 90 dB(A) gives rise to a duty to provide hearing protection. For the first time, limited duties are imposed upon employers where an employee has a daily personal noise exposure in excess of 85 dB(A). At this level of exposure, the employee must be provided, at his request, with ear protectors; the employer also has a duty to make a noise assessment. There are also other requirements, which should be considered in cases where there has been noise exposure after 1 January 1990.

Chapter 8

Limitation

Limitation is often pleaded in deafness cases. Frequently, the plaintiff's cause of action will have accrued more than three years prior to the issue of the writ. The usual principles apply, and it is not proposed to provide a detailed treatise on limitation in this work. In many cases, the plaintiff's deafness will not have manifested itself to him/her until a more recent date. In such a case, the plaintiff can rely upon the "secondary" limitation date, namely the date of knowledge. However, in most cases the court will exercise its discretion, if necessary, under section 33 of the Limitation Act in favour of the plaintiff. Normal considerations will apply and it is not beyond the bounds of possibility that a defendant might be able to prove substantial prejudice, for example if the factory premises have recently closed down so that accurate noise levels cannot be measured.

Chapter 9

By the way ...

Some further information: The careful reader may have noticed a curious feature, when considering the audiogram; see figure 1 in Chapter 4 above. It may be noted that the measurements of frequency do not progress at a uniform rate along the horizontal axis of the graph. This is because each doubling of frequency raises the pitch of sound by precisely one octave. Thus, if we begin with a deep bass tone at 250 hertz, a tone at 500 hertz will be precisely one octave higher. The next octave will be at 1,000 hertz, 2,000 hertz, 4,000 hertz and so on. A pure tone at 8,000 hertz will be precisely five octaves higher than the tone at 250 hertz.

In fact, the measurements would normally be undertaken at 256 hertz, 512 hertz, 1,024 hertz and so on. These are so close to the round numbers as to make no discernible difference. The reason is this: begin at 1 cycle per second (1 hertz). (This tone at 1 hertz, if it could be produced, would be wholly inaudible.) Raise an octave to 2 hertz. Then to 4 hertz. 8, 16, 32, 64, 128 and 256 hertz. And so on. For all practical purposes, 250 hertz equates with 256 hertz. The same, of course, applies in the higher frequencies.

Some further information about decibels: as we have seen, noise pressure level, or noise intensity is traditionally measured in decibels. It is important to note that an increase (or reduction) of noise pressure level by, say, 1 decibel will not produce a uniform increase/reduction in loudness at different noise levels. This is because decibels are a logarithmic set of units, so that every increase in intensity of 10 decibels reflects an increase in intensity by a factor of 10. A sound measured at 80 decibels is 10 times as intense as a sound of 70 decibels. Thus, a sound of 90 decibels is 100 times as intense as a sound of 70 decibels. Extending that same principle, an increase of 3 decibels will double the noise intensity. Thus, 90 decibels is twice as intense as 87 decibels; to increase to 93 decibels is to quadruple the noise intensity at 87 decibels. 96 decibels would be eight times as intense.

Although we have equated intensity (or noise pressure level) with a concept of "loudness", it is necessary to add the following proviso.

Although a sound at 90 decibels is twice as intense as a sound at 87 decibels, the human ear (if it were able to make a judgement) would not perceive the noise as being twice as loud. However, it should be firmly understood that, at the higher levels (say when 90 decibels is exceeded) every additional one decibel is potentially much more damaging than the last one decibel increase.

IN THE MELCHESTER COUNTY COURT   Plaint No. _____

BETWEEN:

A A   Plaintiff

— and —

X Y Z LIMITED   Defendants

Particulars of Claim

1. From about 1964 to 1977 (subject to discovery) the Plaintiff was employed by the Defendants as a machine operator at their premises in the City and County of Melchester.

2. The Factories Act 1961 applied to the said premises.

3. In the course of his said employment the Plaintiff worked within the said premises and was there regularly and persistently exposed to noise created by processes tools and machinery and, in particular, by saws, spindle moulding machines, and other woodworking machinery.

4. As a result of his aforesaid exposure to noise the Plaintiff has suffered and suffers deafness.

5. The Plaintiff's deafness has been caused by the negligence and/or breach of statutory duty of the Defendants, their servants or agents in that they:

(a) caused or permitted the Plaintiff to work in conditions in which he was exposed to excessive and dangerous levels of noise;

(b) used in the said premises tools and machinery and carried out processes, in particular as set out in paragraph 3 above, which created excessive and dangerous levels of noise;

(c) failed to take any or any adequate steps to reduce the noise to which the Plaintiff was exposed to a safe level;

(d) failed to provide any or any suitable hearing protection for the Plaintiff or to take any or any adequate precautions to prevent damage to the Plaintiff's hearing;

(e) failed to give the Plaintiff any or any adequate warning or instruction as to the risk of damage to his hearing by reason of his exposure to excessive noise;

(f) failed to give any or any proper instruction or advice as to the wearing of ear protection and/or any or any proper supervision in and about the wearing of such protection;

(g) failed regularly or properly or at all to carry out medical examination of the Plaintiff's ears and hearing ability;

(h) failed to provide at the said premises a safe and proper system of work and/or place of work and/or exposed the Plaintiff to unnecessary risk of injury;

(i) failed to heed complaints and warnings in terms that noise levels within the said premises were too high and that proper protective measures should be taken. Such complaints had been made at works Safety Committee meetings from about 1969 onwards and fuller particulars may be given following discovery herein;

(j) negligently and contrary to Regulation 44 of the Woodworking Machines Regulations 1974 they failed to take measures to reduce the levels of noise within the said premises and/or to provide suitable ear protectors for the Plaintiff's use;

(k) in the premises the Plaintiff's place of work was not made and kept safe for him in that he was there exposed to excessive noise as hereinbefore set out, negligently and contrary to Section 29(1) of the said 1961 Act.

6. As a result of the aforesaid negligence and/or breach of statutory duty of the Defendants the Plaintiff has suffered injury, loss and damage.

Particulars of Personal Injuries

The Plaintiff, born on 18 October 1940, suffers and has suffered from bilateral noise-induced deafness accompanied by tinnitus. There is a particular loss of hearing in the high frequencies causing difficulty in speech discrimination. The Plaintiff is handicapped in his social and everyday activities. His condition will not improve and is liable to deteriorate with increasing age.

And the Plaintiff claims DAMAGES together with interest pursuant to section 69 of the County Courts Act 1984.

DATED, etc

Index